T0022966

HUMANS
& ANIMALS

WHAT WE HAVE IN COMMON

Albatros

CONTENTS

We humans have long thought of ourselves as superior to animals, because of, for example, our ability to use tools, build complicated structures, use complex language, and experience diverse emotions. For ages, animals were seen as mere machines, driven purely by instinct.

In the 1960s, though, this view began to change. At that time, scientists observing animals in the wild started to notice that animals have some of the same abilities as us. Jane Goodall, for example, observed how chimpanzees caught food with tools such as sticks or stones.

Scientists not only began to observe in animals an increasing number of similarities to humans; they also began conducting different types of tests with them. One such test was the mirror test, which showed that many animals, just like young children, realize from a certain age that the refection in the mirror is not someone else but themselves.

However, some very intelligent creatures, including octopuses, did not pass that test. What could it mean? Well, perhaps nothing at all. In tests, scientists often assess animals using criteria based on human standards, but many animals rely on different senses than humans and perceive situations differently.

Let's focus on what unites humans, not on what makes us supposedly superior to other beings. Although it may seem that humans are a little more advanced in some ways, as no other animal has mastered space travel, written a book, or created a masterful work of art, there remain many areas in which animals are more proficient. Indeed, without animals, which have often served to inspire or assist us, we might not have accomplished some of these achievements.

Animals and humans live in shared communities. We communicate with each other, we form relationships with each other, and we also experience a variety of emotions. Animals feel joy and love and also argue, like humans do. Termites build huge structures in which the whole community lives and works together. Crows can fashion tools to help them overcome difficult situations. Elephants play together and show love for one another, and if a friend or relative dies, they mourn the loss.

Humans can both create the things around them and also destroy things forever. It would be a huge pity to lose the beautiful world of nature just because we consider ourselves superior to other creatures. So let's try to get to know the living beings around us better and treat them with more kindness and respect.

Agriculture has been an inseparable part of human life for many thousands of years. We are very skilled farmers and we grow a diverse range of crops that feed families all over the world. We have all kinds of assistance, from animals to really powerful machines, which give us lots of help with all the hard work. But humans are not the only creatures who can grow food. Among the creatures that have started using agriculture, humans are only in fourth place!

WE FARM

WE USE TOOLS THAT MAKE OUR WORK EASIER AND MORE EFFICIENT.

PEOPLE AROUND THE WORLD MOST COMMONLY GROW CORN, GRAIN, AND RICE.

At first, humans had to rely on their hunting and gathering skills, so as not to go hungry. And when there was nothing to gather or catch, they had to journey to other places.

All that changed around 12,000 years ago, when prehistoric humans discovered that they could grow plants themselves. They began to settle permanently in one place. Thanks to the food supplies!

Gradually, humans learned to breed wild animals. They domesticated sheep, goats, and other cattle. Humans bred animals not only for meat and milk, but also for their help with work in the fields.

6

Humans are amateurs compared to ants of the genus Atta. These ant farmers perfected their skills over 50 million years ago! A convoy of ants carries pieces of leaves to an underground city, where they grow a fungus that they feed on. And it grows like crazy! No wonder—the ants fertilize it with a mixture of leaves chewed into a mushy pulp, ant saliva, and excreta. Besides ants, other creatures also enjoy gardening, farming, and even breeding cattle. Animal farmers are just as good as their human counterparts.

INSTEAD OF TOOLS, ANTS USE THEIR MANDIBLES, WHICH CUT THE LEAVES UP IN NO TIME.

THE ANT WORKERS MAKE THIS TRIP SEVERAL TIMES A DAY.

The dusky farmer fish lives on coral reefs. It maintains seaweed gardens, which it carefully tends by picking out any unwanted weeds. It bravely defends its garden against greedy thieves!

The yeti crab lives at great depths where hot water escapes from the Earth's interior. It grows its food (bacteria) on its hairy claws and harvests it with its comb-like mouth.

Common ants breed aphids much like humans breed cattle. Aphids secrete honeydew, a sweet nectar that ants love. The ants provide protection to the aphids, so they can drink to their heart's content.

Humans are playful creatures, and children especially love to play. Playing is not only fun; it's also extremely important for their development. Through play, we learn new skills, cultivate relationships with others, and get to know the world around us. In the course of our lives, the games change and we develop in all kinds of ways. We are lucky that our childhood is unusually long compared to that of other creatures. It means we have a lot of time to play different games!

WE PLAY

CHILDREN LIKE
PLAYING CHASE AND
HIDE-AND-SEEK.

EVERY CHILD NEEDS
TO PLAY, JUST LIKE
THEY NEED FOOD AND
SLEEP.

Parents play with their children from a very early age. When playing, children use all of their senses, which helps them to develop in all kinds of ways.

Older children use their imagination in their games, because they have more developed brains. A stick can be a sword for fighting a dragon and a soft toy is a great companion for a tea party.

Even adults still like playing games. They are just a bit different from the ones they used to play. Adults like to play board games or card games with their family or friends.

You are most likely to see young mammals engrossed in play, but birds and reptiles are no exception. Animals spend a lot of time playing different kinds of games. Animals sometimes play alone, or with their parents and friends. The most common form of play is fighting or chasing. Young ones explore their surroundings and face unfamiliar situations while playing. It engages and strengthens their bodies and brains. What's more, it's such a good time!

ELEPHANTS CAN COMMUNICATE WITH EACH OTHER. A SHAKE OF THE HEAD IS AN INVITATION TO PLAY!

ELEPHANTS HAVE UNUSUALLY LONG CHILDHOODS, SO THEY PLAY AND ROLLICK TO THEIR HEART'S CONTENT.

Kittens are excellent at playing the hunter. Almost anything can draw their attention. They often catch their prey and then release it for fun. Perhaps they are practicing hunting for the future.

Some chimpanzee girls collect sticks or pebbles to use as dolls. They look after them, cuddle them, carry them around, and put them to bed. They will certainly make excellent moms!

Adult dolphins like to play a clever seaweed game. They pass it to each other in the pod like a ball. It's a fun game and it also helps strengthen relationships between the dolphins.

We have long thought that using tools is a privilege strictly for humans. Thanks to the evolutionary changes in the bodies of our ancient ancestors, such as walking upright on two feet and having skillful hands and a more developed brain, we mastered the skill of tool-making. However, we now know that animals are also able not only to use tools, but to make them as well. Even so, we are still one step ahead of them, as we think in much more complicated ways. And we have invented so many things that have made our lives much easier.

WE USE TOOLS

TOOLS ALLOW US TO PREPARE MUCH TASTIER MEALS.

MAN-MADE TOOLS ARE LITERALLY ALL AROUND US.

From an early age, we learn to use different tools. Gradually, we get better at using them. For example, we first learn to eat with a spoon. Then we move on to using a knife and a fork.

At first, our ancestors weren't too good at using tools. Their abilities were comparable to those of other primates. But as their brains developed and their hands became more skillful, things began to change.

Humans are able to make complex tools, which can make other tools! From simple devices, such as a potter's wheel, to complex machines in factories that churn out thousands of tools each day.

There are quite a few animals in the wild that use tools. And it's not just mammals: the use of simple tools has been mastered by birds, and also fish, crabs, and certain species of octopuses. So, why do people and animals actually do this? Well, they do it to get food, to make their lives easier, and to protect themselves from the dangers of the world around them. Some creatures use tools instinctively; others have watched and learned how to use them. But only the cleverest can make, modify, and refine tools by themselves.

CHIMPS BREAK THE HARD SHELLS OF NUTS OR FRUITS WITH STONE TOOLS.

A TWIG IS GREAT FOR CATCHING TERMITES. LEAVES CAN BE USED FOR DRINKING OR, ALTERNATIVELY, FOR TOILET PAPER.

The little veined octopus lives near the ocean floor, where there is nowhere to hide. So, it often carries coconut half-shells with it. When in danger, it uses them to build a fort, which protects it.

Do we need arms to use tools? Of course not. When many birds and fish find a difficult-to-open treat, they simply take it in their mouth and whack it on a hard surface until it opens.

New Caledonian crows modify things around them to solve various problems. Worms hiding in wood are best pulled out using a twig with a hook at the end. They use their beaks to make the hooks.

Every day, millions of adults leave their homes and go to work. Some of them work in buildings and others work out in the open air. If you look around you, you will see all kinds of different professions. All of them are useful and important, because thanks to them, we make a great community. It doesn't matter if you work as a teacher or a mail carrier. The best is when people enjoy their work. What would you like to do when you grow up?

WE WORK

A POLICE OFFICER

A HOT-DOG VENDOR

A STREET CLEANER

We go to work to earn money and provide our families with food, shelter, and security. We spend a lot of time at work, and that's why we cherish the time we spend with our families.

Many people work helping others. Some people have highly demanding jobs, such as doctors. Before they can start work, they have to become experts in their field.

In creative professions, people's ideas and visions can take shape. Architects can transfer their designs from paper right onto the street and their buildings rise up in every city.

Wild animals may not work in the same sense that humans do, but that certainly doesn't mean they don't work at all. So, what do they do? Usually they look for food for themselves and their families and try to protect themselves from danger. Many animals also have important roles that contribute to the proper functioning of their environment. In the water and on land, you will find inspectors, cleaners, security guards, and gardeners everywhere. If their home happened to be damaged or destroyed, all that work would have been for nothing.

ANIMALS THAT LIVE IN GROUPS, SUCH AS MEERKATS, ALL HAVE THEIR SPECIFIC ROLES.

A SECURITY GUARD

A NANNY

A SUPPLIER

Bird moms have very important jobs: day after day, they provide food and protection for their chicks. They have to do their job really well; otherwise their young wouldn't survive.

Going inside a moray eel's mouth takes a lot of courage. Cleaner wrasse fish operate stations where they give their customers a healthy cleaning. In return, their customers don't eat them!

Beaver dams are not just opulent homes. They contribute to the health of the neighborhood. The dams prevent flooding and drought, and ensure the well-being of other living creatures.

How are human babies different from those of animals? Once we are born, we are totally dependent on our parents, and without them, we wouldn't survive. This is because we are not born fully developed—we have to grow and mature once we have arrived in the world. Our muscles get stronger, our brains get larger, and we develop all kinds of skills. We gradually learn everything that is important. Human parenting is unique in the natural world, as no other creature looks after its young for as long as humans do.

NEWBORNS FEEL SAFE AND SECURE IN MOM'S ARMS.

NEWBORN BABIES ARE HELPLESS. THEY ARE UNABLE TO MOVE OR EAT ON THEIR OWN AND THEY CAN'T TALK.

A mother carries her baby in her belly for nine months before giving birth. After the little one is born, it is looked after primarily by its parents, while friends and family help out.

At first, human babies need the help of their parents for everything. Their parents protect, feed, and carry them, and gradually teach them to become independent.

Some couples are unable to have children, even when they really want them. The solution is to adopt a child who doesn't have any parents. This way they create a new loving family!

There are different kinds of animal parents. Sometimes, it is only the mother who takes care of the young, and sometimes it is both parents. In some cases, the newborns never even meet their parents. Mammals, who take very good care of their little ones, are among the most devoted parents. And it's no wonder, as the mothers feed their young on milk, so they can look after them longer and teach them everything they need to know. These young mammals are often among the cleverest, like apes. Some offspring of other animals are fully developed and self-sufficient almost as soon as they are born and are able to begin independent lives right away.

THE MOTHERS TAKE CARE OF THEIR YOUNG FOR EIGHT YEARS. ONLY WHEN THEY ARE COMPLETELY INDEPENDENT DO THEY HAVE ANOTHER OFFSPRING.

AFTER IT IS BORN, THE BABY ORANGUTAN HOLDS ONTO THE HAIRS ON ITS MOTHER'S CHEST AND LETS ITSELF BE CARRIED, FED, AND PROTECTED.

Seahorse dads certainly stand out in the crowd. First, the mom lays eggs into a pouch on the dad's belly. He then carries the eggs until it is time to give birth to teeny-weeny seahorses!

Many animals can take care of themselves soon after they are born. They wouldn't survive in the wilderness otherwise. Young giraffes can run an hour after being born!

Animals also adopt abandoned offspring. This is usually done by mothers who have lost their own young or who have not yet had their own. Adoption is common among northern elephant seals.

Humans like talking to each other. Thanks to language, we can express our thoughts, feelings, desires, and needs, and pass on information about ourselves and our surroundings. Human language consists of words with meanings, which are composed into sentences that follow certain rules. We are unable to speak from birth and we wouldn't be able to learn our mother tongue without help from others. At first, our language is clumsy, but we soon learn to speak like real experts!

WE COMMUNICATE

WE CAN TALK ABOUT THINGS BEYOND WHAT IS HAPPENING RIGHT HERE AND NOW, AND WE CAN ALSO TALK ABOUT THINGS THAT ARE NOT REAL.

All our words are accompanied by body language: we use gestures, we have a particular posture, and our face reflects our feelings. This helps us understand what others mean by what they say.

We can communicate just as well in writing as we do by speaking. Thanks to written language, we can send letters, emails, and text messages to people we can't see in person.

Some people are deaf, yet they have no trouble communicating with each other. They use sign language. They "talk" with their hands and read people's lips.

You will often read that what separates people from animals is language and the ability to communicate with it. Yet animals communicate proficiently with one another, and they do so without the need for words. Using a combination of sounds, facial expressions, and gestures, they convey everything they need to. It seems, however, that the themes discussed by animals are somewhat limited. They mostly talk about what's going on in the moment. But who knows? Perhaps animals do have complex languages of their own but we have not yet managed to decipher them.

BIRD LANGUAGE VARIES ACCORDING TO THE SITUATION.

SHARP SHRIEKS ARE A WARNING.

CHICKS CHIRP LOUDLY WHEN THEY WANT FOOD.

MELODIOUS SONGS ARE USED IN COURTSHIP.

Many animals use facial expressions, postures, and gestures to show how they are feeling. For example, the facial expressions of horses can show whether they are scared, happy, or feeling curious.

Animals have very highly developed senses. Some rely on smell to communicate, others on touch. Koalas use both; they send messages by means of smell and say hello by rubbing noses.

Some creatures can communicate even in the dark. Fireflies, for example, call out to potential partners by lighting up their bottoms. The message is clear: let's get together!

Some humans, by nature, are rather timid and don't like to draw attention to themselves. Others, however, will take any opportunity to show off. Their worlds sometimes come together, for example, when they are trying to win someone's heart. All of us try to attract the attention of the person we like. We make ourselves look and smell nice for them, and spend time with them in nice places. We'll do anything to grab their attention. Some people lavish gifts, others hope their deeds will do the trick.

WE SHOW OFF

It takes effort to win the heart of someone we admire. A little thoughtfulness may help—a pretty flower or a small gift.

Both women and men try to make themselves attractive for someone they like. Many women use makeup to draw attention to the beauty of their eyes and lips in order to enchant their admirers.

Dance also reveals a lot about a person. Lots of couples like to get on the dance floor together and show off various dances. If they are a good dancing couple, it is a promising sign.

In days gone by, knights sought to win the hearts of the ladies they admired in knightly tournaments. Fortunately, men have abandoned such practices and they don't fight this way anymore.

When trying to find a mate, many animals don't just rely on the heart. Male animals, in particular, must be able to attract a mate in the face of much competition. There are many ways in which animals show off during courtship. Some have to gradually gain the female's attention; others just have to wait for it. If females are not sufficiently interested in the coloring, dance, smell, song, or gift of a potential partner, it is just bad luck. The females go for the best male to start a family with.

BOWERBIRDS BUILD LITTLE WEDDING HALLS, CALLED BOWERS, INTO WHICH THEY ATTRACT FEMALES.

THE BOWER IS DECKED OUT WITH ALL KINDS OF DECORATION. THE MALE WAITS FOR A FEMALE TO APPROACH. IF THE FEMALE ENTERS THE BOWER, THE MALE HAS SUCCEEDED.

Female baboons make themselves attractive in a truly unique way. When they want to attract a mate, their rump swells up and turns a striking red color. Courtship can then commence.

During courtship, peacock spider males seduce females with a dance. They display the colored flaps on their abdomen, wave them, and move from side to side. How could anyone resist?

Sometimes courtship gets out of hand and there is a fight between two males. Bison arch up and push up against each other with their horns. The victor in this duel wins the heart of the female.

Because we humans are inquisitive beings, we learn throughout our lives. We learn things that are essential and things that we need for our adult lives, but we also learn fun things that make us happy, such as playing a musical instrument. We learn the most important basic skills and lessons in life from our parents at an early age. Later, teachers help us learn all kinds of interesting things. However, we also gain a lot of knowledge simply by observing others and then imitating what they do. But if somebody guides us, the chance of us actually learning something skyrockets.

WE LEARN

TEACHERS USE THEIR EXPERIENCE AND KNOWLEDGE TO HELP US LEARN BETTER.

If something bad or painful happens to us, we learn from that experience. Our brains remember that terrible incident and we don't make the same mistake again. Lucky us!

When we find ourselves in a new and unfamiliar situation, we can often work things out by drawing on our knowledge of similar situations in the past. It help us deal with the new situation.

Learning has an influence on us. We associate certain situations with what we have learned. For example, when we think about our favorite food, we immediately get hungry.

Even though animals are born with innate instincts, there are many things they still have to learn. Just like us. However, unlike us, animals don't have to go to school, as all important knowledge is passed on from parent to offspring. When young animals grow up with their family and their species, they pick up everything they need by observing them. When they grow up alone, for example, if they are reared in captivity without their parents, they don't have the same knowledge as their wild relatives. Chimpanzees bred in captivity, for example, are unable to build their own nest for sleeping without the aid of their parents.

In bear families, the mother takes on the role of teacher. The cubs learn from her how to be a bear, which means learning how to find food and how to climb trees and swim.

Animals also learn from unpleasant experiences. If a curious dog doesn't leave a porcupine alone, he'll get a painful lesson. And, next time, he won't mess with any porcupines!

Crows in Japan have learned to use cars as nutcrackers. They throw a nut on the road and wait for the car to run over it. They gather the nuts when the cars are standing at the traffic lights.

If we repeat something over and over again, in time, animals learn to form associations with this activity. When, for example, guinea pigs see their cage door opening, they start sniffing for food.

We all have a talent for something—some of us excel in math; others are good at sports or painting. Plenty of people can cook wonderfully. Still, there are some whose talent stands out above all others. Thanks to an incredible amount of hard work and determination, they have honed their skills almost to perfection. The feats these talented individuals can achieve are awe-inspiringly beautiful. If you have hobbies like these, pursue them wholeheartedly!

MAGICIANS HAVE A TALENT FOR INVENTING WONDERFUL TRICKS. FOR EXAMPLE, THEY CAN CONJURE A DOVE OUT OF AN EMPTY HAT!

WE HAVE TALENTS

Acrobats have bodies like rubber. They can do the splits and somersaults without blinking an eye. Some can even touch their nose with their feet! But it takes much hard work and practice.

Athletes who are better than all other competitors in an event often become world record holders. Some runners are so fast that they could keep up with cars driving in the city.

People who have the talent of being able to imitate others are often great actors. They can impersonate all kinds of characters, be they people, animals, or even inanimate objects.

Although animals don't feel the need to compare their abilities with others, many of them have talents at which only they excel. Animals have not only much better-developed senses than humans, but also different bodies. This means they can do things that people can only dream of. Their optical illusions, their flexible bodies, and the speed at which they move can take your breath away. Let's take a look at some of the wonderfully talented creatures in the animal kingdom. Perhaps they will inspire us and we will learn a few new tricks.

WHEN IT'S NOT IN DANGER, THE MIMIC OCTOPUS TAKES ON A BLAND COLOR THAT BLENDS IN WITH THE SANDY SEABED.

THE MIMIC OCTOPUS IS A REAL MAGICIAN. IN ORDER TO DEFEND ITSELF FROM ENEMIES, IT CAN CHANGE THE SHAPE AND COLOR OF ITS BODY TO MIMIC MORE THAN 15 DIFFERENT ANIMALS!

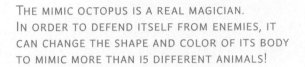

Although owls have fixed eyes, they can rotate their heads to incredible angles in all directions. An owl can watch you, even when it has its back to you.

Even though there are faster runners than the green basilisk, they certainly can't do what it does. When it needs to escape, it runs across a short stretch of the water's surface.

When can you hear in the forest a combination of sounds such as a car starting, an alarm sounding, or a baby crying? When you come across a superb lyrebird. It can imitate any noise it hears!

Even in prehistoric times, humans knew that there was strength in unity. When they cooperated with others, they accomplished much more, and more easily, than if only one person had tried. They were able to overpower large wild beasts, share food among themselves, and build communities. It's no wonder that the idea of cooperation has survived to this day. Working together simply benefits us all—we save ourselves time, share the workload, and achieve so much more.

WE COLLABORATE

DOGS BECAME MAN'S BEST FRIEND MANY THOUSANDS OF YEARS AGO.

DOGS NOT ONLY PROTECT US, THEY HELP US AS WELL. THEY AID THE POLICE, RESCUERS, AND ALSO PEOPLE WITH DISABILITIES.

When people work as a team, they are very effective, whether it's building a house or working in a factory. Every member of the team plays a part in carrying out a task successfully.

Whenever an accident happens, people come together, put their differences aside, and focus on one goal: working together to help the person (or animal) in difficulty.

Many sports, such as football, hockey, and relay races, are team sports. The individual members always try to help their team win. If they don't make an effort, the team won't get very far.

Some animals only look after themselves, and no one else benefits. However, many animals have discovered that if they work with others, symbiotically, they can live a little better. They don't just stick to their own species; they are willing to team up with other animals. The best kind of teamwork is the kind that all the participants benefit from. In the wild, many animals and plants are so closely connected that they could not survive without each other.

Oxpeckers help zebras clean their hair and get rid of ticks. In return for their services, dinner is on the house!

On the African savannah you will find oxpecker birds that are friends with many animals.

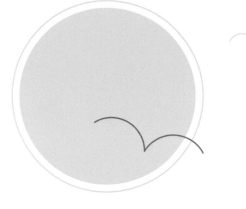

Bees are a shining example of teamwork. To keep the hive healthy, each of the over ten thousand individual bees plays its own predetermined role in the community.

Animals also help each other selflessly. For example, when a member of an elephant herd is injured or a baby elephants falls, the herd will gather around and help out the unfortunate one.

When it comes to food, animals that live together function as one unit. During a hunt, every member of the wolf pack knows its job, so they all can fill their bellies.

If we want to be strong and fit and stay healthy, there are some important things we need to pay attention to. We certainly need plenty of exercise in the fresh air and also a healthy diet, but we shouldn't neglect proper hygiene either. Cats are a good example. They spend hours cleaning themselves with their tongues. Taking care of ourselves also means having a proper rest, whether it be slumbering in fluffy duvets or relaxing in the pool.

WHEN WE'RE OUTSIDE FOR LONG PERIODS OF TIME, WE NEED TO PUT ON SUNSCREEN SO THAT WE DON'T GET BURNED.

WE TAKE CARE OF OURSELVES

When we get sick, we need a lot of rest so that our body can fight the illness. Different kinds of herbs can also be a great help. And when all else fails, we need to visit the doctor.

Even a seemingly ordinary activity, such as washing your hands properly, helps prevent all kinds of diseases. Lather your hands with plenty of soap and then wash every nook and cranny.

Sometimes we simply need to relax. Some people like to read a book; others prefer to take a bubble bath. Relaxing and getting enough rest are very important for our health.

Animals are almost always on the move. They spend every moment in the fresh air, and they maintain a healthy lifestyle, as they only eat what is good for them. Still, they also need to take care of themselves. But there are no medicines, cosmetics, or beauty salons in the wild. So, how do they do it? Well, they use all the things they have around them. It's no coincidence that nature's products are the most effective. And it's possible that people have learned a few tricks from animals, such as which herbs are good for an upset stomach.

RHINOS PROTECT THEMSELVES FROM THE HARSH AFRICAN SUN BY ROLLING IN MUD. DRY MUD ALSO PROTECTS THEM AGAINST INSECTS.

When animals eat something bad, they have to deal with it themselves, as they can't go to a doctor. Chimpanzees chew bitter herbs, dogs swallow grass, and parrots eat clay to get rid of a stomachache.

Bats take really good care of themselves. They clean their wings and bodies with their tongues. And where their tongues won't reach, they use their wings! Bats wet their elbows to clean their little ears.

Animals also like to be pampered. Hippos can't resist an underwater spa, where small fish clean their skin and even their teeth. After this procedure, the hippos lounge around contentedly.

Humans have always built homes where they can live together in safety with their families. Whether it's a cave, a hut, an apartment, or a grand villa, home is a place that we can return to and spend time together with our loved ones. Some people live in city apartments, while others prefer to live in houses in quiet villages. Even today, there are indigenous tribes in the world that have very modest living arrangements. For some people it is normal to wander without staying in one place. These people have portable homes that are easy to put up anywhere.

WE HAVE HOMES

In cities, there are tower blocks and skyscrapers where lots of families live.

Although we humans are clever builders, we often inhabit preexisting places adapted for our needs. In Tunisia, for example, to this day, some people live in cave dwellings.

Indigenous peoples live in harmony with nature, so their houses are simple and practical, built from the materials they find around them. The Inuit, for example, build their homes from blocks of snow.

People who wander from place to place are called nomads. Desert nomads carry their homes with them on camel caravans. Their homes are tents, which are easy to put up and fold up again later.

Not many animals live with their families in open, insecure places. Most have homes where they are protected from exposure to the weather and their enemies, and where they can raise their young in peace and safety. Many animals use natural structures such as caves, crevices, and tree hollows. Many crafty creatures inhabit abandoned burrows or nests that were built by others. We cannot overlook the ingenious builders who can build homes of such magnificence that humans can only look on with envy. And for those who are always on the move, home is where their family is.

THE MOUND IS INTERWOVEN WITH CORRIDORS AND CHAMBERS, WHICH EVEN HAVE VENTILATION.

A TERMITE MOUND IS, IN FACT, A HUGE CITY THAT CAN RISE TO A HEIGHT OF OVER 26 FEET.

IT IS INHABITED BY MILLIONS OF TERMITES.

When animals lack building skills, they do not despair. This raccoon family made a home in an empty tree hollow. If it hadn't been available, they would have easily found another natural place to live.

The tiny harvest mouse weaves its house from little blades of grass and suspends it above the ground between stalks of tall grass. In this remarkable little home, it rears up to eight young.

Some animals, mostly those that travel, have more than one home. Many birds fly to warmer climes for the winter months, after which they return to their normal residence.

29

Children have other children all around them. Some have only one or two friends, others have lots. One thing is for sure: for children, making new friends is a piece of cake! But the older we get, the smaller and more permanent our circle of friends becomes. We tend to make friends with people who have similar values and interests to our own. Some of our friends are closer to us than others, and our best friends stand by us through thick and thin. They're so important to us that they're like family members!

WE HAVE FRIENDS

WE CALL THE FRIENDS WHO ARE CLOSEST TO US BEST FRIENDS.

Sometimes people make friends as children and the friendship lasts into old age. Friendship can help prolong our lives, simply because we are at our happiest among friends.

Friendships don't always work out. We sometimes have arguments and hurt each other's feelings. We don't have to become enemies, we just go our separate ways and the friendship ends.

Can people set their differences aside and become friends again? Of course we can! It can sometimes be quite simple: we just need to talk through our feelings and work things out.

Although there are many loners in the animal world, plenty of animals enjoy the company of their own species. In other words, they have friends. These animals include primates, cows, elephants, bats, flamingos, and even snakes! Nevertheless, some seem to pick out a few individuals from the group with whom they have a closer friendship. Why do they do this? Well, because they benefit from the relationship in some way—for example, it makes them safer or ensures a greater supply of food.

AS WITH HUMANS, NOT ALL FLAMINGOS GET ALONG WITH EACH OTHER. GROUPS THAT ARE NOT ON FRIENDLY TERMS AVOID EACH OTHER.

IN A FLOCK OF MILLIONS, YOU'LL FIND SMALL GROUPS OF FOUR OR FIVE FLAMINGO FRIENDS.

Friendship and lifelong love is relatively rare in the animal kingdom. Even so, there are some couples who are so devoted to each other that they simply cannot live without each other.

Unlike humans, animals cannot choose their enemies. Nature has decided that some animals are food for others. The roles of the hunters and the hunted are simply predetermined for animals.

Sometimes, seemingly incompatible animals can be friendly toward each other, particularly when they gain something from their friendly relationship, such as more food or protection.

Every day, we experience a whole range of feelings inside us. We may feel troubled, happy, afraid, or surprised. Emotions can be read from our facial expressions, physical reactions, and body language. You could say that emotions show our feelings on the outside. When we feel happy, we laugh. When we are sad, we cry. It may sound simple, but emotions can also be deceptive. Humans are able to disguise them. A person may laugh, even though they feel sad inside. But, compared to animals, we have a wonderful gift: the ability to speak and express thoughts and feelings in words. So let's make the most of it!

WE HAVE EMOTIONS

CHILDREN DON'T HIDE THEIR FEELINGS OR EMOTIONS. YOU KNOW AT ONCE WHEN THEY ARE ANGRY OR HAPPY. THEY ARE ALWAYS VERY HAPPY TO SEE SOMEONE THEY LOVE.

Fear is one emotion that is inherent in all creatures. When we are afraid, our hearts pound faster, and we instinctively seek to protect ourselves from the source of danger, sometimes by running away.

When someone hurts us or things don't work out for us, we feel anger. It's a powerful and complex emotion, but it helps us set boundaries. It's better to say why we're angry than to break something.

When we lose someone we love, we feel grief and sorrow. Some people cry, others might not show any emotion. This is called mourning and it helps us come to terms with our loss.

For a long time, scientists thought that animals were only driven by instinct, unable to feel or express their emotions. But now we are learning that animals in fact do experience emotions in a certain way. Unlike humans, animals are unable to express them in words, but both pets and wild animals have feelings and show them outwardly. When they are happy and content, their bodies are relaxed. When they are afraid, they cower. And when they are angry, they steel themselves, ready to strike.

DOGS ARE FULLY ABLE TO EXPRESS THEIR JOY. JUST LOOK AT THEIR BODY LANGUAGE!

THEY JUMP UP, WAG THEIR TAILS, AND LICK THEIR COMPANIONS IN WELCOME.

When animals feel threatened, they either run away or stay frozen to the spot. When an animal is trembling, in a crouching posture, with its ears flattened down, we know that it is afraid.

Playing with an angry cat is no fun. If its back is raised, its tail is erect, and its fur is bristling, it is better to leave it alone. A cat won't think twice about using its claws to fend off its enemy.

When magpies lose one of their group, their companion's death does not go unobserved. They stand and mourn by the body, as if at a funeral. Giraffes, elephants, and gorillas grieve in a similar way.

The human body consists of a skeleton connected to muscles. In cooperation with our brains, these components perform a marvelous trick: they make our bodies move. As we grow, we need to move in various ways that test and strengthen our bodies. We progress from simple walking to more demanding disciplines, such as running, jumping, climbing, and swimming. Although our bodies are different from those of animals, we can do similar things. Nevertheless, human bodies have their limits. They are adapted to our way of life and cannot match the specialized movements of expert animals.

WE MOVE AROUND

AS THE BODIES OF BABIES DEVELOP, THEY GRADUALLY IMPROVE THEIR ABILITY TO MOVE: FROM CRAWLING AND TODDLING, THEY WORK THEIR WAY UP TO WALKING.

Among primates, humans are unique in that we walk on two legs. Our bodies have become fully adapted to this kind of movement, so we can stand and walk, but also run and jump.

We are used to being in water. After all, a baby develops in its mother's belly in liquid. Although we learn to swim properly over time, small babies are immediately comfortable in the water.

We have invented bicycles, skates, and skis, which allow us to perform special movements. But inventions such as hang gliders or airplanes allow us to move in ways that are beyond our physical abilities.

Unlike humans, animals make use of a really wide range of movements, and the structure of the bodies of individual animal species is really diverse in the natural world. The whole and individual parts of their bodies have adapted so that they can survive as successfully as possible. Although the basic building blocks are similar, as many animals' bodies consist of skeletons and muscles, the way they are put together is influenced by many different factors, including the environment in which the animal lives. Water dwellers tend to have bodies with fins, whereas creatures of the air usually have wings. Either way, animals make full use of their ability to move.

SNAKES THAT LIVE IN THE DESERT MOVE SIDEWAYS. THEY DON'T SINK INTO THE SOFT SAND OR GET BURNED BY IT.

EVEN WITHOUT LEGS, IT IS POSSIBLE TO MOVE. SNAKES MOVE IN WAVES, WHEREBY THEIR BODIES BOUNCE OFF THE UNEVEN GROUND.

Only a handful of animals move on two legs. Emus can run fast, and kangaroos are excellent jumpers. Some primates and bears can stand on their hind legs but move about on all fours.

Animals have a variety of tricks for moving about in the water. Fish move by flexing their bodies. Sea turtles use their flippers as paddles and rudders. And frogs and water birds have webbed feet!

The distinct body structure of some animals' bodies allows them to move in ways that humans can only dream of. Birds, bats, and insects fly, and some squirrels and snakes even glide through the air.

© Designed by B4U Publishing for Albatros,
an imprint of Albatros Media Group, 2022.
5. května 22, Prague 4, Czech Republic
Author: Pavla Hanáčková, Illustrator: © Dasha Lebesheva
Printed in Ukraine by Unisoft.

ISBN: 978-80-00-06357-7

All rights reserved.
Reproduction of any content is strictly prohibited without
the written permission of the rights holders.